Tring Personalities

by

Wendy Austin

First published February 2000
by Wendy Austin,
18 Priory Gardens,
Berkhamsted,
Hertfordshire.
HP4 2DS

ISBN

0-9537924-0-4

Design and Typesetting
by Design Conscious
Hemel Hempstead
Tel: 01442 397072

Printed by Alpine Press Limited,
Station Road,
Kings Langley,
Hertfordshire.
WD4 8LF
Tel: 01923 269777

TRING PERSONALITIES

CONTENTS

LIST OF ILLUSTRATIONS

Over the centuries Tring and its surrounding villages have produced their share of varied personalities. This selection of 20 Profiles includes just some of the most interesting.

They have not been chosen for Influence, or for Wealth, although a few were born in favourable circumstances. Among the most intriguing are some of the poorest who lived in the area, and there were others who began life in very ordinary conditions, and became noteworthy because of their resolve and ability.

The group contains many of sterling qualities, and others of flawed character. The Profiles include soldiers, clergymen, scientists, writers, politicians, tradesmen, as well as a 'witch', and a courtesan.

A volume of this type relies upon books and articles of many sorts which have been carefully preserved. Without such records these Profiles could not have been written, and for this help I am grateful. Where possible I have indicated sources of information, and am especially indebted to Jill Fowler and Mike Bass for passing on to me the results of their own researches from past editions of 'The Bucks Herald'.

My thanks go also to those who have supplied incidental details which may otherwise have been lost. Most of the illustrations are taken from items in my collection, but others have been loaned to me to copy and I am grateful to George Bradding; Martin Craven; Wanda Farey; Hodder Headline Group; Geoffrey Hughes; Olive Lovegrove; Alan Rance; Miriam Rothschild; the late Dorothy Ward; Rhoda and Lewis Whitehouse.

Readers will surely be grateful to Alec Clements who has taken a sharp pair of secateurs to my rambling prose.

W.M.A.
February 2000

JOHN BROWN 1795-1890

Brewer, Sportsman, Entrepreneur - all descriptions which could be applied to John Brown, a larger-than-life character who spent most of his long life in Tring. John was born in Okeford Fitzpaine, a village in Dorset, and the son of a yeoman farmer. It is not known why he chose Tring in which to settle in 1826, but he at once set about making his mark, and soon summoned his brothers to join him. Samuel, his twin brother, assisted John in his business enterprises, and William, the youngest, established a firm of land agents which is still trading today as Brown & Merry.

John began well by founding the Tring Brewery in the premises at 24 High Street, the sign of which can still be seen in stone lettering above the archway. As his business grew, he acquired or built nine public houses in Tring and district. He designed the new houses in a distinctive late-Regency style, easy to recognise by the large front porch, supported by two substantial white columns. Other examples which he owned, and which carry similar distinctive columns, are *The King's Arms* in King Street, *The Greyhound* at Wigginton, and *The Royal Hotel* at Tring Station.

This last is a particular reminder of John Brown's business timing and flair. When the London to Birmingham Railway was built in the mid-1830s, John at once identified the opportunity for an hotel adjacent to the newly-opened Tring Station. At that time the land in this area was owned by the Comte d'Harcourt of Pendley Manor, who had recently fled to Paris to escape the intrusion of the canal and railway, both now crossing his estate. Approaches were made to him by John but the Comte refused to sell, so John journeyed to Sunningdale to see the Comte's agent, and persuaded him to talk to his master. In this he was successful, and the erection of a tactfully-named *The Harcourt Arms* resulted. At a later date the hotel received its present name of *The Royal Hotel.*

This fine edifice was soon a base for John Brown's interests in hunting and steeplechasing. The Earl of Lonsdale kennelled his harriers at the hotel, and later the drag hounds of the Tring & District Farmers Association were also kept there until the 1920s.

The Brown twins were keen steeplechasers, and continued to be so until a few years before their deaths, each living into his nineties. It is recorded that they took part in the first Aylesbury Steeplechase, John Brown riding his horse 'Confidence'. The first of the Tring Steeplechases was held in 1844, and again John was a keen participant. The route chosen included Pond Close, Icknield Way, Gamnel, Tring Grove, and Marshcroft; with Dinner at 4 p.m. in *The Harcourt Arms*. Unfortunately it must be said that the treatment of the horses used for this sport would be completely unacceptable today. No regard was paid to the exhaustion of the animals, or to how much their legs could suffer on frozen ground.

John Brown was a hard man in other ways too. Tring soon recognised him as one of those rare folk who 'get things done'. He was appointed Overseer of the Parish, and finding its finances in a parlous state, he added a half-crown rate five times in the one year - a levy unheard of in those days, as was the summons to every person who hesitated to pay.

The Royal Hotel. c.1994

The Brown Family flourished in Tring for some generations. John and his wife Mary had a daughter Emily, and two boys Herbert and Frederick. On their father's death, the two sons inherited the Brewery and the nine public houses, but their trading activity came to an end in 1898 when Frederick sold the whole business to Locke & Smith of Berkhamsted.

The King's Arms. c.1902

John Brown died in 1890, and was buried in a coffin made from a large oak grown on Tom's Hill. A fine stained glass window to the memory of both John and William can be seen on the east wall of the south aisle of Tring Parish Church.

Sources

'Records of Old Times', J K Fowler 1898
'That Tring Air', Arthur MacDonald 1940
'The Sporting Life', 1904
'Hertfordshire Countryside', 1973

'Let not poor Nellie starve'. These were some of the most famous last words ever uttered, and addressed by King Charles II to his heedless brother, James. For the short time that Nell (Elinor) Gwyn survived her royal lover she did not go hungry, but her financial wings were clipped severely, and contemporary reports note that she had all her silver plate melted down.

For seventeen years Nell enjoyed the favours of Charles, often fighting a fierce rearguard action to maintain his interest in the face of strong competition from several other royal favourites. But she was quite equal to the task, displaying her diminutive figure and pretty round face to good advantage, even captivating Samuel Pepys. He (admittedly always susceptible) described her as 'pretty witty Nelly'.

Nell first came to the attention of Charles II some time before 1668 when he was attending the Drury Lane Theatre. She is usually described as an actress and orange-seller, but one source states that she peddled pickled herrings - although this could have been the spiteful satire common at the time. She may have been born in Herefordshire, but her youth was spent in her mother's drinking establishment in Drury Lane, thought by many to have been a bawdy-house. It is true that by the time Nell met Charles she had a very impressive list of lovers, but by 1671 she had two sons by Charles, and had been 'set up' in a small house at the east end of Pall Mall.

Just when, or even if, Nell stayed at Tring is not truly known. What is certain is that in 1669 Charles gave 'the Manor of Great Tring' to Henry Guy, who was a favourite courtier and a trusted finance minister. One of Guy's duties was to oversee regular payments to the royal mistresses. 1670 and 1671 were the years of Nell's greatest power over Charles, so it seems likely he could have placed her under Guy's protection at Tring, although his reasons remain obscure. It might have been at the time of her pregnancies, or to escape an outbreak of typhus in the City. Local legend persists that Nell lived in 'Dunsley House' (a property owned by Lady Throckmorton (née Lake) of Aston Clinton, sited on the edge of Tring Park in the area of the present Memorial

Gardens). This house was described as 'Commonly called *Elinors*', and the north walk from the Mansion to Dunsley House was called 'The Nell Gwyn Avenue'. Dunsley House was later added to the possessions of the ever-acquisitive Henry Guy.

Tring mothers told their children for generations 'Run round Nell Gwyn's monument whilst holding your breath, and an orange will fall off the top'. This adage referred to the obelisk at the centre of the *etoile* in Tring Park. [The number of times you needed to run round seemed to vary between three and seven.] Another fragment of Tring folklore claimed that Nell waited impatiently for sight of Charles's carriage and gazed wistfully down the London Road from the summer house built on the side of the Oddy Hill. Well, if she did, it could not have been from the existing summer house, because both this and the monument are classic 18th century structures, erected some fifty years after Nell was at Tring.

Nell Gwynne Monument, Tring Park.

Nell Gwyn's Monument, Tring Park. c.1910

It can be seen that the common belief of 'Nell at Tring' is flimsy in Fact, but strong in Hearsay. But nothing undermines a true Tring-ite's belief that she was undisputedly here.

Nell was fiercely ambitious for herself and for her surviving son by Charles, and although her firstborn, Charles Beauclerk, born in 1670, was created Earl of Burford and later Duke of St. Albans, Nell herself never acquired the honours she craved and thought she deserved.

When eventually the title Countess of Greenwich was about to be conferred upon her, this was frustrated by the death of Charles. Nell was illiterate, but she did make a Will which was signed with a shaky 'E.G.' In November 1687 she died of apoplexy (nowadays known as a stroke) and is buried beside her mother in the grave-yard of St Martin's-in-the-Fields.

Sources

Dictionary of National Biography, Vol.1
'King Charles II', Antonia Fraser 1979

In 1996, at a special ceremony, the grave of James Osborne at St. Bartholomew's Church in Wigginton, was re-dedicated. Relatives, villagers, members of the Royal British Legion, representatives of regimental associations, and many others - all came for a service to honour Private Osborne. Wigginton was showing its justifiable pride in its local hero.

Twenty years before the Boer War, a previous conflict had occurred between the settlers and the British. At that time the general unrest was compounded by Boer trekkers moving inland in search of settlement areas, and Zulus and other tribes warring with each other. The British had originally occupied Cape Town, and needed to strengthen their position in the country. The troubled situation further north caused unease, and in 1879 the British marched into Zululand. On 22 January two disasters struck: 1,400 soldiers were massacred in a camp at Isandhlwana, and later the same day the British position at Rorke's Drift was attacked by 4,000 Zulus, this famous engagement resulting in the award of eleven V.Cs.

Far away in England weighty decisions were taken that the Zulus must be crushed, and reinforcements were hastily despatched. These included the 58th Regiment (2nd Battalion, Northants Regiment). Among them was James Osborne, aged 22. Landing at Durban in April the army marched north to Ulundi where the Zulu Royal Kraal was destroyed. Later the Zulu impis were also defeated. These actions further alarmed the already-embittered Boer settlers who decided upon a war of independence against the British.

In February 1881, the 58th Regiment was garrisoned at Fort Napier in Wakkerstroom, Natal, where one day some native tribesmen were sent out to forage for the company's horses. This group was ambushed by over forty Boers, and a party of mounted soldiers hastened to their relief. During the action six men were cut off some three to four miles from the fort, and in a critical position under heavy fire from three sides. Four managed to get away, including James Osborne, but the remaining pair, Bennett and Mayes, were wounded and unable to escape. When

James Osborne and John Mayes

beyond reach of enemy guns James reined in his horse, and realised that his friend Mayes was left behind. He urged a watching civilian to lend him a fresh mount, but was refused. So without further delay James turned his own exhausted horse and rode back through the continuing gunfire to rescue Mayes. When he reached him, he slung Mayes' rifle over his own shoulder, pulled Mayes into the saddle with him, and once again galloped through a hail of fire. Providence must have been with the two men, for Mayes later told how one of the flying bullets had struck the stock of James's rifle, close to the grip, and even the Boers later commented that they had never seen a braver act.

This outstanding courage earned James Osborne the Victoria Cross, presented to him by Lieut-General Smythe in the presence of all the company at Fort Napier. James survived many more encounters, including a heavy defeat for the British, when he saw action again in the battle of Majuba Hill. This violent struggle, in which the commander General Colley was killed, was described by the 'London Gazette' as disastrous for the British, and resulted in an armistice which finally recognised the independence of the Transvaal.

James Osborne's army service ended in 1883, and he returned home to Wigginton with a pet monkey named 'Jocko'. James was born in Osborne Cottage in Wigginton Bottom, and his family had lived in the village for many generations. He continued the tradition by marrying a local girl Rhoda Collier, became an estate-worker for Lord Rothschild, and lived on Clay Hill in a Rothschild cottage which he called *Majuba*. Sadly, his later years were not easy, as in 1913 he suffered a stroke which left him partially paralysed. During 1920 King George V hosted a special garden party at Buckingham Palace in honour of holders of the Victoria Cross, and when he learnt that James was disabled, the King ordered that a car be sent to Wigginton to convey him to London.

As time went by James had to depend upon his family for his care. On fine days he could be seen sitting outside his door, awaiting the return of his dog, often sent with money in its mouth to buy tobacco at the village shop. When James finally died, full military honours were accorded to him, and his flag-draped coffin was borne on a gun-carriage from *Majuba* to the burial ground at St. Bartholomew's Church. James Osborne's story ends with misfortune. His VC medal was loaned to his regiment, and during World War II various regimental valuables were stored in Belfast. The entire collection was lost to enemy bombing, and the medal was never found. But the memory of an extraordinarily brave man still endures.

The Victoria Cross

Sources

James Osborne's family
The Illustrated London News, April 1881

Opinions seem to differ as to Arthur Pope's merits as a clergyman, but what does emerge is an interesting character, both principled and eccentric. He was born in London, son of a clergyman, educated at Christ Church, Oxford, and attained his B.A. in 1863 and M.A. in 1865. Arthur was Vicar of Tring in 1872 to 1881, and is remembered chiefly for his initiative in funding and building New Mill and Gravelly Schools, St. Martha's Church, and in addition a new clergy house in Park Road named *The Furlong*. He provided the last two buildings following his predecessor's firm expectation that Tring would increase greatly in size at its west end. It has never done so.

Mention was made of these benefactions at an 1897 Jubilee celebration, and an extract from Arthur's rejoinder, astounding the worthies of the parish, gives a flavour of the man. 'These things had to be done, the congregation did not come forward to do them. I was not going round begging for money, and I did them, to the detriment of my children's education. The parish should be ashamed of themselves for allowing me to do it'.

Nobody doubted that Arthur Pope ministered conscientiously to his flock, but various contemporary versions survive of his preaching style. Cussans, the County Historian, states 'Mr Pope was an excellent man, but very unfitted for his position. He was a ritualist, and his parishioners for the most part low-churchmen. A man with less learning and more tact would have suited Tring better. For six days a week he locked himself in his study to compose a sermon for Sunday which, when delivered, might as well have been in Hebrew so far as the great majority of his hearers was concerned. He was much too learned for his congregation, and had not the gift of "preaching down" to them'. Other accounts have Arthur thundering from the pulpit on subjects as various as cottage economics and hygiene.

After he resigned the vicarage of Tring, he continued to live at *The Furlong* and often preached for his brother clergy in the surrounding villages. Tring people are reputed to have flocked to hear what Arthur would say, but this report seems at variance with Cussans' opinion. One Christmas he exhorted his flock 'Pay your bills! How can you expect your tailor to pay his men if you don't pay him? Here is the first thing you can do to help your fellow creatures'. It obviously did not occur to Arthur that the regular services of a tailor were beyond the wildest expectations of most of the working-class folk in Tring and the villages.

As to be expected he took his duties as parish priest extremely seriously. In preparing candidates for confirmation, each was called many times to his house, and he imparted his whole soul and spiritual experience to them, often with lasting effects on their entire lives. He provided Tring with a temperance Working Men's Club in what was previously a public house, *The Dolphin* in Frogmore Street. This is now remembered in the name of the town's shopping precinct. He was fond of lecturing the working men on one of his favourite subjects - hygiene. 'Don't put your sweaty clothes and boots in your children's bedroom. You put a

St. Martha's Church, Park Road. c.1900

nail in your child's coffin every time you do so. Put your boots up a tree, down a well, anywhere except the bedroom'.

Arthur's high-mindedness did not prevent him from participating in the activities of local society. An account of July 1909 gives a wonderful picture of an impressive Edwardian wedding, when his only daughter, Muriel, married the curate of Tring. A lengthy account describes the ceremony at Tring Church; who was there; and what the chief participants wore. When the happy pair returned to *The Furlong* we are told that the Gravelly school children were drawn up in line outside and they cheered the bride and groom very loudly. The railings of the school had been

Reverend Arthur Pope

festooned lavishly with flowers, evergreens, and flags. Mr and Mrs Pope had hosted an elaborate 'At Home' for Tring's principal residents the previous day. A long list of wedding presents is given. Let us hope the young couple considered themselves particularly fortunate to receive a silver teapot, coffee pot, jug and sugar basin from Lord and Lady Rothschild, and an antique mahogany whatnot from Mr and Mrs John Bly.

Towards the end of his life Arthur had to bear some bitter experiences. The first struck in 1912 when his son Hugh, an eminent mountaineer, was killed attempting a solitary rock climb in the Pyrenees. He was buried at Orthez. Mr and Mrs Pope again had to brace themselves in 1918 when, only three months before the end of the Great War, their eldest son, Harold, was killed whilst serving in France where he had been at the front since June 1915. Captain Harold Pope was a brave man, having won both the M.C. and Bar. It is to be hoped that the parents' strong Christian belief sustained them in both of these tragedies.

Arthur lived until 1921, being buried by the wall of the old cemetery behind the Parish Church, and so passed from the scene one of Tring's most colourful Victorian characters.

Sources

> *The Bucks Herald, July 1909 and September 1918*
> *'That Tring Air', Arthur MacDonald 1940*
> *'A Professional Hertfordshire Tramp', John Edwin Cussans.*

Much has been written about both Emma's distinguished husband and her eccentric son, but rather less of the lady herself. This may be because, although she was surrounded by grand style, Emma did not believe in flaunting her position as wife to the richest man in the British Empire. Great wealth was something she was born to, and accepted as normal, but on one point she was markedly different to many others of high social standing - she believed her good fortune should carry serious responsibility in all her actions. Emma was born a Rothschild, one of seven daughters, her father managing the Frankfurt branch of the family banking firm. She grew up a Lady in every sense of the word. Her bearing was upright, her manner gracious, and her erudition was formidable, for she could speak three languages without a trace of accent. Although she tended to be serious, this was overlaid by a disposition which was very generous, and her personal conduct was beyond reproach.

At that time it was often usual for Rothschild cousins to marry, sometimes as a family duty, but in this Emma was very fortunate, for she fell into true love with her English cousin, Nathaniel. They were married in Frankfurt, but spent their first five years in London. Then in 1872 they moved to Tring Park. The splendid park and house had been acquired at auction by Nathaniel's father, and furnished and equipped in every detail. Emma was not consulted in any way, and had her first glimpse of what was to be her home for the next 63 years on the day she moved in! She was at once enraptured by the house and its surroundings at the foot of the Chiltern Hills, and this feeling remained with Emma for the rest of her life, for she never considered living in any other property. As her husband's political and business influence grew, it became necessary to 'improve' and enlarge the house. The exterior alterations were not especially pleasing, and the inside was considered by some to be a mixture of the very beautiful, and the immensely ugly, even though the house was furnished in the grand manner. But neither Emma not her husband viewed these matters as of major importance. As head of all Rothschild interests Nathaniel had to give much time to many subjects, and his position in the financial world also caused him to be consulted in political situations. As his commitments kept him so much in London he left the care of his Tring responsibilities very largely to Emma.

This was a task Emma responded to with dedication. Whilst her three children were still young, she become intensely interested in the welfare, health and education of Tring women and children. She had the rare gift of being able to really listen, which so raises the confidence of others. By 1879 she had entries in her own account book of some 400 local charitable causes that she personally supported. In addition she subscribed to 177 worthy charities in and around Tring, including convalescent homes, temperance societies, lying-in societies, needlework classes, and scores of Parish Church and Nonconformist projects. She sponsored dancing and wood-carving classes, firework displays, reading and club rooms, one of which she built at Hastoe. The whole community recognised that she cared greatly, for she gave her time to appear personally at special events such as bazaars, displays, and Church Lads' Brigade entertainments. One project close to her heart was the erection in the 1890s of *Louisa Cottages*,

LOUISE COTTAGES AND MUSEUM, TRING.

Louisa Cottages, Park Road. c.1903

named after her mother. These eight attractive small houses were occupied by retired employees on the Tring Park estate. The catalogue of good work continued with the founding in 1900 of Tring Nursing Association at *Nightingale Cottage* Nurses' Home in Station Road, now rebuilt as a modern clinic.

Lady Rothschild in Coronation robes

Although a devoted family person, Emma nevertheless disapproved of her raffish brother-in-law, Alfred (of Halton Manor), because of his ambiguous relationship with a married woman of doubtful repute, who was never received at Tring Park. Alfred, always a humorist, got his own back posthumously when, in his Will, he left his strait-laced sister-in-law an extremely valuable oil painting of a decidedly risqué subject. The shocked Emma gave it away very hurriedly.

In 1900 Lord Rothschild had planned for the future by buying the Champneys estate at Wigginton, intending it to be a future dower house for Emma. Although a widow for 20 years, in the event she never needed it, and chose to remain at Tring until her death at the age of 91. She died peacefully, and as she would have wished - in her bedroom overlooking the beech woods along the ridge in Tring Park.

Tring Park. c.1905

Sources

'Reminiscences', Lady Battersea 1922
'Dear Lord Rothschild', Miriam Rothschild 1988

Sir Robert Whittingham was Lord of the Manor of Pendley when the house was to the east of the present Pendley Manor, thus siting his property just within the Parish of Aldbury.

For five hundred years Sir Robert and his lady have lain with hands folded in prayer and with open eyes gazing at the ceiling. They started life, or should we say 'death', in the chapel of Ashridge Monastery. When that institution was disbanded in the sixteenth century, a descendent of Sir Robert Whittingham arranged for the splendid monument to be re-sited at Aldbury. They now repose in the Pendley Chapel of the 13th-century church of St. John the Baptist.

The tomb is within a Parclose (carved stone screen), the only one of this type in the Chilterns. The floor is covered with tiles, also removed from Ashridge, and Sir Robert's feet rest upon a strange wild man holding a club. On the wall of the chapel a rather confusing inscription carries the history of the Whittingham family.

Robert Whittingham was the third of three Sir Roberts, inheriting the estate in 1452. In his father's time Pendley had been a thriving community, being described as 'a great town, with work for more than 13 ploughs . . besides divers handicraft men, shoemakers and divers others'. In 1440, anxious to create his own deer park and warren, the second Sir Robert enclosed 200 acres, an action which almost certainly did not endear him to the inhabitants of Tring and Aldbury. Sixty years later an account by someone called Boorder of Tring Grove states 'the town was afterwards cast down and laid to pasture by Sir Robert Whittingham who built at the west end there as the town sometimes stood'.

The third Sir Robert must surely have had little time for local concerns, being appointed Keeper of the Wardrobe to Margaret of Anjou, queen of the ill-fated Henry VI. He later became a soldier actively engaged in the vicious battles of the Wars of the Roses. As a prominent Lancastrian supporter, accounts show him fighting at the battles of Wakefield in 1460 and St Albans in 1461. After the latter he was knighted by the Prince of Wales.

Following the triumph of the Yorkists, a price of £100 was put on his head. The Battle of Towton crushed the Lancastrians and Sir Robert, lucky to escape with his life, fled at once to join Queen Margaret in Scotland, accompanying her south again for the seige of Carlisle. After the Lancastrian defeats, along with others he was attainted of treason by Parliament in 1461 and imprisoned in the Tower, his estates, including Pendley, being confiscated.

About this time Sir Robert's only daughter, Margaret, married John, son of Sir Ralph Verney. (After Sir Robert's death, in consideration of Verney's loyal record, the attainder was posthumously lifted from Sir Robert, allowing John and Margaret to inherit the estates. Thus Pendley passed to the Verney family for five generations.) Both families are remembered in Tring by roads named after them.

After Henry VI's brief restoration, Sir Robert continued his allegiance to Queen Margaret, and fought for the cause at the Battle of Tewkesbury. He is said to have died gloriously, refusing to release the Royal Standard from the firm grasp of his mailed fist. After such a turbulent life, let us hope Sir Robert Whittingham remains undisturbed in Aldbury Church and continues to enjoy his contemplation of the ceiling.

Sir Robert Whittingham

Sources

Victoria County History, Vol. II
Guide to Aldbury Church, 1965

Keith Simpson was the Home Office Pathologist in the decades following World War II, and his forensic investigations involved him in many celebrated murder cases. At that time the shadow of the scaffold lay across the outcome of sensational trials, and the accounts of all murders were followed with macabre interest by the public. Many of these are remembered still today - Neville Heath, John Haig, James Hanratty, Lord Lucan, Dr. Bodkin Adams, and most grisly of all, John Christie and Timothy Evans. In all Keith Simpson took a key part.

On his own admission he was by nature a reserved man (at least in early life), and this may have applied too in his local dealings. In a profession so often in the public eye, and connected with matters of great notoriety of an unpleasant sort, he knew it was wise to keep a low profile. Curiosity about such activities is probably best avoided before it can surface.

Professor Keith Simpson C.B.E.
(Photo: 'Simpson's Forensic Medicine' by Bernard Knight)

Keith lived in a beautiful spot under the hanging beech woods at Dancer's End. Tring folk walking in Holland's Dean, or looking from a distance over to *Dancer's End Lodge,* would point out the house to visitors, and say in suitably awed tones 'That is where Professor Keith Simpson lives'. In fact, not many knew what he looked like, but despite this he was a household name at that time.

Keith was born in Brighton, the son of a respected General Practitioner, and was brought up in comfortable circumstances. He was educated at Brighton & Hove Grammar School, and Guy's Hospital Medical School, which he entered at the early age of 17. He had wanted to attend University first, but his father considered it unnecessary, envisaging for his son a straightforward career in general practice. Soon however Keith decided upon a specialist branch of medicine, one which was not particularly popular or well understood at the time.

Not many young doctors would choose to take up the study of the dead, especially those diseased, mutilated, and sometimes even dismembered; and to find themselves in derelict premises, the bedrooms of dead prostitutes; and at the scene of graveside exhumations at daybreak. Keith Simpson thrived in these harassing conditions where it was imperative to be observant, meticulous, and above all accurate, and to be able to deal with a complete cross-section of those in all walks of life. His work also brought him into contact with the most eminent judges, lawyers, and detectives of the day.

A list of his achievements is almost endless. He rose to become Professor and Head of Department of Forensic Medicine at Guy's Hospital. He was both a foremost Lecturer and an Examiner in this subject, in this country and abroad. He travelled to all areas of the world in response to requests for assistance in every aspect of his subject. As he had a strong belief that special knowledge should be shared he was responsible for numerous text books, and his publications include 'Modern Trends in Forensic Medicine', 'Doctors' Guide to Court', 'The Investigation of Violence', as well as many others. He also edited 'Taylor's Principles and Practice of Medical Jurisprudence', the 'bible' on which all pathologists rely.

Keith Simpson's life contained its own share of tragedy. His first wife, Mary Buchanan, a nurse at Guy's by whom he had three children, died of multiple sclerosis at an early age. In 1956 he married his secretary, Jean Scott-Dunn, and lost her too, this time to cancer after 20 years of extremely happy marriage. Much later and towards the end of his life he wed a third time, Jane Thurston the widow of a colleague.

Generally his private life was his own, in contrast to the notoriety of his public dealings. Keith Simpson confessed he greatly enjoyed his house and garden at Tring, using them as a haven of quiet, far away from court-rooms, mortuaries, police stations, and the often sordid locations to which his profession took him. Keith died at the age of 77.

A fitting obituary would be to reflect on the contribution that any human being makes during his or her life. If it is considered that the correct person should be punished for crimes such as assaults, rapes, and appalling murders, then Keith Simpson must surely be regarded as one of the most important inhabitants that our district ever had.

Sources

'40 Years of Murder', Keith Simpson 1978
'Who was Who' 1981-1990

THOMAS GLOVER 1822-1914

Villains often make more interesting reading than saints, and it is very difficult to write a profile of a character such as Thomas Glover. He epitomises one's idea of a true Victorian worthy, as few people have served the town of Tring more faithfully. His appearance suited the part, for he dressed in black and sported a flowing white beard which reached to his waistcoat. His disposition was kindly and genial, and his principles sincere and unyielding.

Both of Thomas's parents came from Surrey, but he was born in Tring. His father Richard was so respected that 67 members of the congregation of the Akeman Street Baptist Chapel in 1813 asked that he become their pastor. His ministry was so successful that by 1832 a completely new chapel was built, able to hold a congregation of 850.

Thomas did not follow his father's profession, but chose to go into partnership with Joseph Gates at No. 19 High Street. They are listed in a trade directory of 1851 as Grocers and Tallow Chandlers. The business prospered and Thomas was able to marry, and to support six children to a good standard. His continued success enabled him to live in one of the most attractive houses in Tring - No. 4 Park Street.

The mainspring of his life was a staunch Nonconformity, which he had surely inherited from his father. Thomas was a Free Churchman to the core, liberal in thought, and true to the principles of civil and religious liberty. He made no enemies, and won for himself the respect of many who held widely differing views from his own. He was also closely associated with the Akeman Street Baptist Chapel throughout his life, and for 70 years he was the Sunday School teacher there. Such establishments had tremendous influence on the scholars who attended in Victorian times, and the effects of this teaching stayed with many for the rest of their lives. In the earlier days he conducted a Bible Class for young men, and Mrs Glover held similar classes for young women. When his beloved wife died he continued the task alone. Later he married again, became Superintendent of the Sunday School and Deacon of the Chapel.

In 1908 came a special celebration, when a grateful congregation paid tribute to Thomas's long years of unbroken service. A delightful party was held at *Frogmore*, the home of his great friend, the banker Frederick Butcher. He received a splendid present which took the form of a silver epergne with detachable vases. No doubt the second Mrs Glover enjoyed the fiddly task of dusting this elaborate centrepiece, having to remind herself each time of the esteem which had inspired the gift.

Thomas participated in other worthy activities of the town, being a member of the Local Board, and a Guardian of the Poor, and he travelled regularly to Berkhamsted for meetings of these bodies. He was a Trustee of Tring Consolidated Charities for many years, and took part in the annual distribution of tickets for coal and for bread. He was known to be generous with his own money, as a contemporary account notes that 'the villagers round about Tring will never cease to remember his name gratefully as one whose heart and pocket were ever open to them'.

Thomas enjoyed fine health right to the end of his long life, but frailty in his last years led him to rely on a good friend to push him around Tring in a bath-chair. In 1914 he was laid to rest in

Frederick Butcher, Revd. Colls, and Thomas Glover
in the latter's garden of No. 4 Park Street

the graveyard behind the Akeman Street Chapel, and his tomb is marked by a simple rough-hewn granite headstone. An impressive memorial to his father, Richard, stands on the grass in front of the chapel. Thomas Glover would not be suprised to know that the Baptist Church in Akeman Street still flourishes, but would be amazed that his grocery business at No. 19 High Street is now the town's main Post Office.

Thomas Glover's life was threaded through with Goodness, and there is no known criticism about him. Of very few indeed can such a comment be truly made.

No. 19 High Street, Thomas Glover's grocery business. c.1920

Sources

'The Bucks Herald' archives
'A History of Hertfordshire Baptists', David R Watts 1986

Mention was made of Henry Guy in 'Tring Personalities No. 2 - Nell Gwyn', but Henry deserves a profile in his own right, as he lived in Tring for 33 years and made his mark in other ways too. His qualities of self-seeking, acquisitiveness, and sycophancy cannot be admired - but it must be remembered that he was a politician.

He was born in the parish of Great Berkhamsted. His mother, Diana Elizabeth Wethered of Ashlyns, died at the age of 90, and is buried under the new altar in the chancel of Tring Church, Henry arranging a memorial tablet in her memory.

Henry Guy was admitted to the Inner Temple in 1652, but soon adopted politics as a profession. He spent some time at Christ Church, Oxford, and was created M.A. Later he held an excise office in the north of England, and ingratiated himself with the electors of the Borough of Hedon in Yorkshire. In 1670 he was elected its M.P., serving seven terms until 1705. He presented to the borough a silver cup, salver, and very fine mace, and in 1693 he erected 'a very large and convenient town hall' for its inhabitants. This fine building is still in use, the original police cell being the Town Clerk's office.

Henry first enters the story of Tring in 1669 when, on the death of Queen Henrietta Maria, he obtained a grant of the Manor of Great Tring from her son. On this estate he built an elegant house, from the design of Sir Christopher Wren, 'and adorned it with gardens of unusual form and beauty'. How he was able to do this is open to speculation as, according to popular rumour of the time, the costs were borne by his pickings from the Treasury. Henry was ideally placed for this, for in 1679 he was appointed Secretary to the Treasury, and payments from public funds passed through his hands until 1688. It is documented that he was in charge of secret service accounts for both Charles II and James II, and even until the time of William III. (As mentioned in the profile of Nell Gwyn, some of these 'secret services' seem to be payments of maintenance and pensions to the royal mistresses.)

It is recorded that when one Henry St. John first came to Court, Henry warned him 'to be very moderate and modest in applications

Henry Guy

for friends, and very greedy and importunate' when asking for himself. Henry seems to have acted on this principle too and it paid off handsomely. Certainly Henry Guy's property at Tring impressed no less a person than Daniel Defoe. Travelling through

Tring Park House built by Henry Guy

the country he writes 'At Tring is a most delicious house, built *à la moderne*, by the late Mr Guy, who was for many years Secretary to the Treasury'. But the account continues with strong criticism of Henry, and a pæon of praise for the villagers of Wigginton. 'There was an eminent contest here between Mr Guy and the poor of the parish, about his enclosing part of the common to make his park;

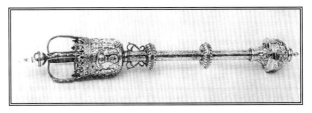

Hallmarked: London 1669. 3 feet 8 inches long.
Inscribed: *'The gift of Henry Guy of Tring in the County of Hertford, Esq.'*

... Mr Guy took a parcel of open land called Wigginton Common; the cottagers and farmers opposed it ... they rose upon him, pulled down his banks, forced up his pales ... this they did several times until he was obliged to desist.'

Henry did in some measure carry out his obligations to Tring as Lord of the Manor. He endowed a curacy for Tring Church in the sum of £20 per year, and in around 1680 renewed the Market House. It was decreed that on Fridays straw plait be sold in the mornings, and corn in the afternoons. This unlovely structure which stood in the High Street immediately in front of the Church, was demolished in 1900 - 'unwept, unhonoured, and unsung' according to the Parish Magazine of the time. The market bell Henry provided was saved for Tring's new Market House on the corner of Akeman Street.

In 1680 Henry acquired from Catherine of Braganza a lease for 30 years of the Manor of Hemel Hempstead, and in 1690 William III dined with him at Tring Park. The year 1695 saw Henry's fortunes take a tumble when he was committed to the Tower for accepting a bribe of two hundred guineas. He was forced to resign his position, but seems to have emerged unscathed, as he left £100,000 - an enormous sum in those days. He died in 1710, but had by that time left Tring, having sold his estate here in 1702.

Sources

> *Dictionary of National Biography, Vol.1*
> *'A Tour through the Whole Island of Great Britain', Daniel Defoe 1724*
> *Hedon Local History Society*

Joseph Budd was not wealthy, not titled, nor did he achieve renown either nationally or locally. He was a likeable easy-going man and a competent tradesman, but so were many others. What makes Joseph different is that he was interested in everything local, and more importantly 'he wrote it all down'. From his accounts emerge a fascinating picture of late-Victorian Tring seen through the eyes of someone born and raised in the town.

His writings were not restricted to personal reminiscences, and in the late 1960s he set out a reasoned argument why Tring should not be annexed by Buckinghamshire - a suggestion that had been revived at that time. In his essay Joseph traced the origins of Saxon Tring from 571 A.D. He stressed that the tribe who settled in Tring were East Saxons, had always been so, and that although the Tring 'bulge' appears on the map to be an intrusion into West Saxon territory, it is not in fact so. The frontier was always clearly recognised at the time, and a space of common land was kept between the two areas. Joseph's account was sent to the Town Council. Whether or not it had any bearing on the ultimate decision is not known, but the fact remains that Tring is still firmly in Hertfordshire thirty years later.

Joseph Budd came from a long-lived family, and he can remember at the age of four being taken to see his great-grandmother who had been born in 1788. He was born in Akeman Street when his father was sixty years of age and his mother forty, saying his parents were 'wonderful to me'. Joseph senior is described in *Kelly's Directory* of 1869 as trading at No.64 Akeman Street as a Marine Store Dealer, a strange description in an inland place like Tring. This probably meant a trader in general commodities, and is borne out by Joseph remembering as a boy being taken by his father to Ashridge House kitchens. This was a weekly visit to collect kitchen waste, including dripping. On one of these trips Joseph senior also bought and picked an entire apple crop from one of the estate orchards. Another activity was a brisk trade in rabbit skins.

The business must have prospered for Joseph enjoyed a comparatively privileged upbringing in those days of general poverty. He tells us he was looked after by a nursemaid during his infancy, and first attended a private school. Later he went to the National Schools in Tring High Street, obviously showing a keen desire to learn, and making good progress.

Joseph's childhood was spent in an Akeman Street very different from the one we know today. On the corner of Park Road stood *The Jolly Sportsman* pub and also *Williams Place*, a row of cottages. All these were swept away when *Louisa Cottages* were built in 1893. He remembers the demolition of the farm buildings which were opposite, and the erection of the Museum. Great excitement was caused when six zebras arrived at Tring Park. These were at first set free among the emus and kangeroos, but proving too wild, they were moved to a small field in Hastoe Lane. Later they were broken to harness, which worked tolerably well, but only if using a small horse as one of the team of four. Life was lived much more in the street, and diversions included visits from German bands, Russian dancing bears, fire-eaters, and contortionists. Travellers plied their trades outside; these included the mat-mender, the umbrella-mender, and the fly-paper man wearing one of his products as an advertisement - wound around a battered top-hat.

In 1899 a less happy event in Akeman Street was a severe outbreak of typhoid. Deaths resulted and schools were closed. The disease was not well understood at the time, and contamination by 'carriers' was not generally recognised. Bad drains and wells were blamed, and Tring UDC organised a supply of disinfectant powder which could be collected free of charge. Water from wells was tested and most, except Rodwells Brewery, were condemned and the lids nailed down. The remedy of connecting cottages to the Mains water supply was not well received, people grumbling about the extra 2d. on their weekly rent charge.

Another of Joseph's accounts explains that 'Gravelly Furlong' was an area of fields which is now Langdon, Charles, King, and Queen Streets. The ancient name describes a stony substance called 'hurbeck' which was unearthed by the ploughs during the medieval period. By 1859 scattered cottages and houses had been built, seemingly with no coherent street plan. After 1860 more and more building took place, and this led to the lay-out we see today. Several businesses flourished in this area including canvas-weaving shops owned by the Cato family, and Hilsdon's Engineering Works near the western end of King Street - the machinery being driven by a steam engine. *Gravelly House* was the premises of an undertaker, and next door No.55 King Street was Joseph Budd's home, from where he ran a successful coal merchant's business in a yard taken over from Alfred Fincher in 1929. During World War II he combined his business activities with enthusiastic participation in the Tring Home Guard contingent.

In 1911 Joseph had married his childhood sweetheart, who as a little girl sat next to him at school, Joseph being instructed to 'look after her'. They lived contentedly at 55 King Street, a house

Joseph Budd and his wife in 1936

without modern conveniences, for well over 40 years. It is pleasant to record that Joseph and his wife celebrated their Silver, Golden, and Diamond Weddings - in all a remarkable 67 years of happy married life.

Joseph Budd in 1943

Sources

The writings of Joseph Budd
'Evening Echo' December 1970

MRS. HUMPHRY WARD 1851-1920

Mary Augusta Arnold was born in Hobart, Tasmania, where her father was an Inspector of Schools. When Mary was four years old the family returned to England and her education included an unhappy period in a boarding school, and then to a finishing school in Bristol. At this point she was considered as educated as a Victorian girl should be, and she then joined her family in Oxford. Because three brothers had been sent to universities, Mary always resented the fact that her education was less complete. Helping with domestic tasks, and minding younger siblings was not Mary's idea of time well spent, and as soon as she could she applied herself to writing items with a studious content.

In 1872 Mary married a don, T. Humphry Ward, a union which was to prove enduring and happy, but in which Mary was to be the dominant partner, although she was always known professionally as Mrs Humphry Ward. The couple prided themselves on their modern ideas, and this may have been why, unusually for those days, only three children followed. Mary clearly had no more time for child-bearing, and applied herself to her early ambition to be a novelist. Her first great success came in 1888 with the publication of 'Robert Elsmere', a book in which her own religious beliefs (an emphasis on practical Christianity rather than on mystic dogma and ritual) were stated vehemently. Her publisher had expressed doubts about its appeal, and prepared only 500 copies, but the novel was an enormous success and sold over a million copies, at home and in America. This could have been due in part to an excessively laudatory review from none other than Mr Gladstone.

Mrs Humphry Ward was now 'launched' upon the literary scene, a career which produced over 30 major works, plus countless reviews, articles, essays, as well as speeches. On the strength of her success, the Wards sought the ideal country estate, and found it by chance in Aldbury. In 1892 they rented, and later bought, *Stocks House* which was to be their dearly-loved home for the next 28 years. Neither of them had brought any money to the marriage, but they still adopted a style of living taking every penny which Mary earned.

Even in those days of cheap labour, running a country estate was an expensive affair, and together with financial calamities caused by their son (see Tring Personalities No.12), this led to Mary becoming a writing machine, even during her many spells of bad health. As time went on, and in the best tradition, she was often found swathed in rugs, reclining on a *chaise longue,* relying on an

Stocks House. c.1910

array of Victorian pain-killing drugs, and attended by a companion and an unmarried daughter, Dorothy.

In spite of her troubles Mary had to be in vigorous writing form. A few weeks before the Wards moved to Aldbury, a shocking event had rocked the Tring area. Two game-keepers had been murdered by poachers on ground belonging to *Stocks* estate. Mary used this as part of the plot for her next novel 'Marcella', which is loosely based on Aldbury. She was fascinated with local life and often drove her pony-cart into the village, to converse with elderly folk. From these talks she learnt about the local cottage industry, and weaved the story of the decline of the straw-plait trade into 'Marcella'. Following the success of this book, Mary wrote her next short novel in 15 days - 'The Story of Bessie Costrell', which also drew upon a recent village incident.

Novels followed at regular intervals and Mary's breadth of social vision and characterisation caused her to be called 'the second George Eliot'. By 1905 she could claim plausibly to be the most famous living novelist, and even the mighty Tolstoy stated that she was England's greatest artist in fiction. Her books were translated and read everywhere - on the Continent, in Scandinavia, in the Balkans, and in the Colonies. In America no other English writer had so devoted a public. Many critics there sneered at her work, but nothing they said halted the sale of her novels by the hundredweight.

Why is it then that her reputation, unlike George Eliot's, has not endured? Perhaps it was the tendancy she had of 'preaching' to her readers; or maybe the sheer turgidness of some of the books; or the out-moded values? Whatever were the reasons, the fact remains Mary Ward is not read today, and is an almost forgotten name.

Arguably in this modern age she should be remembered for a different reason. To this day, a plain building at 42 Queen Square, Holborn, bears the name *Mary Ward House*, but few entering the doors have any idea why it is so called. In 1897 Mary's strong social conscience stirred her to act on behalf of the poor of London. Two other settlements for the underclasses were already in existence, but Mary had her own ideas, and she combined these

Mrs. Humphry Ward at Lake Lucerne in 1912

with her own strong streak of egotism, to form another settlement. Having taken the decision she moved with great speed, forming an influential non-sectarian committee, and embarking on a fund-raising lecture tour which took her all over the country. The Duke of Bedford was prevailed upon to make over a large plot of land on the south-east corner of Tavistock Square, and she also persuaded an elderly philanthropist, Passmore Edwards, to back her. The settlement sponsored a wide mixture of adult education and of recreation, and it included a gym - an innovation at that time. The key impact came with the rapid increase in the children accepted. By 1902 more than 1,200 were being taken care of while their parents were at work. Mary's best success came with her pioneering ideas for handicapped children. A specially equipped ground-floor area was set up for those who, in some cases, had never before been able to attend any school. Great care was given to diet, and much produce was sent to the settlement from the *Stocks* kitchen gardens and orchards. Mary took little direct part in dealing with the children, but she was much more than a mere figurehead, for without her driving fund-raising energy the operation would soon have foundered. Between 1888 and 1898 it is estimated that she earned £45,000 from her novels, and raised at least a similar amount for her settlement. All this activity was woven into a life which had to include periods of invalidism; foreign travel; and social entertainment at Aldbury of the great and the good.

One of her greatest challenges came towards the end of Mary's life. In 1908, on a visit to America, she had met Theodore Roosevelt. He so admired her work that seven years later, in 1915, he asked her to write a series of essays explaining to the American audience the vital reasons for England's war effort. Mary visited factories, the fleet at Invergordon, and, accompanied by Dorothy, even the war zone near Ypres. The result 'England's Effort' was published in American newspapers. Views expounded by Mary seem hopelessly out of date today, but at the time her well-written and shrewd propaganda got the desired result.

Mary Ward finally succumbed to the ailments that had plagued her for so long. She died peacefully in London, at a time when she was yearning to be back in *Stocks*. Her wish was granted after her death, and she was carried on a hand-bier to Aldbury church by the *Stocks* gardeners. The funeral was a mixture of the simple and the grand - local boys sung in the choir, and an address was given by Dean Inge. From Buckingham Palace a message of condolence was received. There was one person remaining unmoved, the genius Virginia Woolf, who had never hidden her doubts about her fellow writer. She wrote in her diary one week later 'Poor Mrs Humphry Ward ..... shovelled into the grave and already forgotten'. Unfeeling as this comment was, it did contain a grain of truth. It is kinder to remember Mary by the words of Clough carved on her tombstone:

> 'Others, I doubt not, if not we,
> The issues of our toil shall see,
> And, they forgotten and unknown,
> Younger children gather as their own
> The harvest that the dead has sown.'

Mary Ward House, Tavistock Square. c.1996

Sources

'The Life of Mrs Humphry Ward', Mrs G M Trevelyan 1923
'Hertfordshire Countryside', December 1969
'Mrs Humphry Ward', John Sutherland 1990

ARNOLD WARD M.P. 1876-1950

Although Arnold Ward was not born with a silver spoon in his mouth, it was at the very least silver-plated. His parents were not wealthy, but well-educated and creative, with impeccable family connections in the fields of literature and education. In fact they named their only son after his mother's illustrious grandfather, Dr. Arnold of Rugby School.

At the time of Arnold's birth, his father Humphry was a tutor at Oxford University. (When he married he had to forfeit his more senior position as Fellow.) Arnold was the middle child, with an older sister, Dorothy, and a younger, Janet. The family soon moved to London and later to *Stocks House* at Aldbury when Humphry became the art critic for 'The Times' - in his wife's opinion a lowly position for a man of his abilities. Mary Ward did not waste time regretting her husband's shortcomings, but instead diverted her energies to promoting her own considerable talents, as well as becoming fiercely ambitious on behalf of Arnold. Her hopes of him were to be sadly misplaced many times over, but Mary was by no means the only mother to view a son through rose-tinted spectacles. Until her death in 1920 Arnold probably remained the most important factor in her life.

In the early years Mary had reason for her maternal pride, for Arnold was an exceptionally bright child, and showed promise in many subjects. After a year at Uppingham, he won a King's Scholarship to Eton. Only four months later his proud mother could tell relatives 'Arnold has done brilliantly'. He continued to excel, and in 1891 won the Consort's German Prize, and inherited from his father a talent for Greek and Latin verse. He was good at all sport, enjoying golf and cricket, and was chosen for the College wall-game team. In 1895 he was picked to play for Eton against Harrow. Mary Ward's cup overflowed when Arnold won a scholarship to Balliol College, Oxford. With hindsight, his glittering school career did augur some dark prophetic moments, for he showed some inclination to what was viewed as schoolboy indiscretions. Although Arnold got 'squiffy' once or twice; overspent his allowance; showed signs of insubordination; none of this was regarded as too serious. It was more ominous that he seemed to have mis-spent, or lost, the cricket XI's funds when treasurer. In this last misdemeanour he was bailed out by his devoted sister Dorothy.

His mother must have been placated when on leaving Oxford he gained a double first, and she could see Arnold as a future Prime Minister. He had made useful social contacts, and had become a great friend of Raymond Asquith, son of the statesman. To encourage her son's dazzling new acquaintances, his mother arranged for both a cricket pitch and a golf course to be constructed at *Stocks*. The world now seemed to be at his feet, but somehow things did not progress. An attempt to win a Fellowship at All Souls' College failed; a spell as a journalist in Egypt ended with quarrels with his superiors; and a request to fight in the Boer War was stifled by his doting parents. It was now decided that Arnold should read for the Bar. Although he passed the exams without difficulty the work bored him.

By 1905 Arnold was 30, with no established profession, and still being supported by his hard-working mother. The end of the year saw an upturn in his fortunes. He was taken into chambers as a pupil, and adopted as Liberal Unionist candidate for a constituency in Wiltshire. He spent much time with the Asquith family, and on the strength of his new prospects, considered proposing to Raymond's sister, Violet. He told his parents of his intention, but what exactly happened is not clear. Perhaps Violet said 'no', but whatever the reason Arnold remained a batchelor.

Much effort was put into Arnold's election campaign by the entire Ward family, and he dutifully espoused the policies favoured by his mother, especially support of Tariff Reform, and resistance to the Female Suffrage movement. The electorate may have sensed all this, for the result was a crushing defeat. Nothing daunted, Arnold stood again as a Liberal Unionist, this time for Watford (conveniently near to *Stocks*). The committee bluntly asked 'are you prepared to pay your election expenses and to subscribe to the funds of the West Herts Unionists?' Arnold was (as long as his mother gave him the money), and he was duly adopted. It was around this time that Arnold's behaviour caused his parents serious

Arnold Ward M.P.

concern. For some time he had been playing bridge for large stakes at the famous Portland Club in St. James's Square, and at this same time he lost his place in the law firm after disputes with colleagues. All these 'difficulties' had to be put to one side as the election campaign began. At the meeting of Unionists in Tring in December 1909 Lord Rothschild endorsed Arnold in his speech, and Mary again threw herself strenuously into her son's campaign, writing letters, paying for a male secretary, and offering the services of the long-suffering Dorothy. This time he won with a majority of 1,551. Mary and Dorothy were rewarded by often being invited to the House, lunching on the terrace, or listening to debates. But all the old worries started to return. Arnold began to fall out with powerful Unionists in his constituency, and evenings at the Portland Club continued. By 1913 the situation was truly serious when he broke the news to his horrified parents that he had run up gambling debts of many thousands of pounds, and had no means of paying them. To save their son's honour, the money had to be found, so Mary and Humphry sold much of their property in Aldbury, namely Barley End, Tim's Spring, and Aldbury Nowers. The balance of the money needed was found when Mary also signed away the copyrights of all her works of fiction.

In spite of Arnold's many solemn promises to his family that he would renounce gambling for ever, the same problem resurfaced in Cairo during his World War I army service with the Hertfordshire Yeomanry. Again, he was rescued by his parents. In his military career he was undistinguished, and although he was now a mature 40 years of age Arnold was never able to rise above the lowly rank of lieutenant, serving time in various army backwaters. His gambling and drinking continued, and he complained of imaginary grievances by his fellow officers against him. His conduct was considered so unacceptable that his regiment refused to have him, and Arnold was transferred to the Reserve Territorial Force. Bad reports of their M.P. reached Watford from local men serving with honour in the Herts Yeomanry and matters were not helped by his behaviour when he was on leave. On one evening he failed to turn up at two meetings arranged at Tring and Berkhamsted, leaving his embarrassed sister to handle the situation. His absences were reported tersely in 'The Bucks Herald' of the time. The inevitable crunch occurred when the constituency requested Arnold's resignation in 1917, but allowed him to complete his term to the next election, presumably out of respect to his mother.

After Mary's death in 1920 Arnold moved to the south coast, and he then made a living from journalism. He died in 1950 and is buried in a grave beside his parents in Aldbury churchyard. Afterwards the ever-loyal Dorothy sorted and burnt all the surviving records of his financial and career difficulties.

How was it that a man born with advantages of birth, a first-class brain, a splendid physique, and good health, should fail to fulfil any of his early promise? Was it due to his indulgent mother, or to his rather weak father, or to some inherent flaws in his own character? Nobody can really say, but all must surely agree that Arnold Ward's story of wasted talents is a sad one.

Sources

'Mrs Humphry Ward', Enid Huw Jones 1973
'Mrs Humphry Ward', John Sutherland 1990

Here is the story of Arthur Gutteridge, a very ordinary man of Tring, who loved horses, and worked with them for over forty years. Fortunately, his good memory has preserved for us some anecdotes from a vanished way of life. His father Ted, born near Gloucester in 1857, had moved to Tring as a young man, and married a local girl. Arthur was born in 1886. Ted found work on the Tring Park estate as an odd-job man, but must surely have been 'talent-spotted', for whilst Arthur was still a small boy Ted became a groom - a much superior post to his previous work. His pay at seventeen shillings a week was two shillings more than ordinary workers, although all at Tring Park thought themselves very fortunate, for Lord Rothschild always paid a shilling a week more than the usual local rate.

His Lordship had been told that the quality of heavy horses on the local and tenant farms was quite low, and being most interested in modern farming methods, in 1887 he bought the five-year-old 'Thorny Tom', a massive Shire stallion from the Fens, which cost him 500 guineas. This was acquired to sire offspring in the Aylesbury and Tring district. In those days the normal stud fee was four guineas, but Tring Park tenants were charged only one guinea. Lord Rothschild became increasingly interested in these magnificent creatures, and set up a stud farm in Duckmore Lane.

Lord Rothschild's Shire Horse Stud, Duckmore Lane. c.1910

To provide more rich grazing for the growing number of animals, three large fields were bought at Broughton Pastures, out on the main Aylesbury Road. The stud also supported its own blacksmith, Bert Christopher.

At the age of 12 Arthur Gutteridge joined his father at the stud, at a princely sum of four and sixpence a week, but that was sixpence more than he would have been paid elsewhere. Arthur admits he was more or less expected to do a man's work, although at that time he was so small he needed to stand on a gate to bridle the horses. He also sometimes had to run errands. One Sunday morning in 1901 at Wilstone, the champion mare, 'Alston Rose' gave birth to a foal. When it was seen to be ill, Arthur was sent on his old cushion-tyre bicycle to tell the vet at Aylesbury. After his long ride Arthur was fed with lemonade and cake, but his journey was in vain, for the foal could not be saved. As Arthur grew older one of his tasks was to help in 'travelling the stallion' round local farms. This operation entailed the tricky business of assisting over-excited male horses to serve mares, and this could be quite dangerous work, for sometimes the stallions were completely unmanageable. Such horses had to be castrated and then given very much less exciting routine farm tasks.

Another exacting job of Arthur's was that of collecting new young horses from Tring Station and returning with them to the Stud. Aware that the horses were very valuable, it worried him that the journey along Station Road and through the town could upset them after their long train rides. In 1904 he collected both a filly and a yearling in one trip, the latter, 'Childwick Champion', turning out to live up to his name by siring many future prize winners.

Arthur remembered that the blacksmith's work could also be hazardous. Many of the Shires would allow nobody but Bert Christopher to shoe them, and more than once he was shot clear out of the farrier's shop when a horse suddenly snatched its foot away. One particular stallion was sold to a stud in Lancashire. It turned out that once there he would not tolerate anyone near his feet. In desperation Bert was sent for and thereafter always travelled to Lancashire to carry out this task.

A Shire stallion at the Stud Farm

All things come to an end, and when Lord Rothschild died, the dispersal sale of the country's most famous Shire stud caused great interest, and record prices were attained. The stud farm continued independently under Tom Fowler, the previous manager.

None of this affected Arthur, who had previously become apprenticed to Jim Goodson, the farrier at 54 High Street, Tring. He said that Jim may have had difficulties in getting his business established because he was a chapel-goer, and in those days people assumed all Nonconformists voted Liberal. When it was known that Jim was a Conservative all was well! When Jim reached 80 years of age, Arthur took over the running of the forge, and trade boomed during the years of The Great War when hundreds of soldiers were billeted in Tring. Arthur recalled he sometimes made 200 shoes a week, and said he remembered horses by their feet more than by any other part of them. One Shire was so bandy in his hind legs that Arthur put lumps of metal on the outsides of its feet rather than shoes. He considered that a mare named 'Kerry Clanish Maid' had the most perfect feet he ever saw, and he kept one of her shoes as a souvenir for the next 40 years.

Arthur married in 1928, the year his father died. He carried on shoeing horses until 1940, but when War help was called for he entered a munitions factory and worked for 11 years until his retirement, although he admitted that the work bored him. Arthur Gutteridge's most fondly remembered times were those of his long-ago youth at the stud farm, and because of his affection for a good employer he hung a photograph of Lord Rothschild in the smallest room in his house.

'Belle Cole' champion mare in 1908, with her foal.

Sources

'The Shire Horse', Keith Chivers 1976
'Horse and Driving', Autumn 1978
'Heavy Horse and Driving', April 1981

In the 17th century the term 'bigwig' meant a man of substance, and therefore one who could afford to wear a sizeable periwig. One glance at the remarkable monument to Sir William and Lady Gore in Tring Parish Church tells us immediately that his elaborate and expensive head-covering showed that he must have been a very Bigwig indeed.

Looking more closely at the memorial we see that Sir William and his lady recline on some rather uncomfortable marble drapery, and have done so since 1707 when their devoted son erected the tomb, originally in the Church chancel. Sir William is discoursing, probably at length, with a graceful gesture of his hand, but Lady Gore has the appearance of finding her distinguished spouse a trifle tedious. By any reckoning this enormous edifice must be thought a little elaborate as a testimonial to a man who lived less than six years in Tring.

Sir William Gore

Sir William bought Tring Park in 1702 at a time when Hertfordshire was very attractive to wealthy Londoners seeking country residences. In those days the River Thames had fewer bridges, and areas north of the river were more accessible than those in the south. During the 17th and 18th centuries London merchants were prominent among those buying property here. Besides many other activities Sir William was a member of the Mercers Company, and served two terms as Master in 1695 and 1697. There were numerous facets to his illustrious career, many of which grew from his first appointment in the City of London where he was made Alderman for the Coleman Street ward.

In October 1692 he was knighted at the Guildhall by William III, and another high point came when he was elected Sheriff of the City of London, followed by the supreme office of Lord Mayor in 1701/2. His procession and pageant must have been splendid indeed, including Mercury (Speed in Business), Neptune (Mercantile Power), and the Spirit of Enterprise. (We are inclined to think nothing notable in Trade occurred until the 20th century arrived.) In the same year (in the quaint terms of the 17th century) Sir William 'over-egged his pudding' when he stood as Tory candidate for the City of London, for in this he failed. Perhaps the electorate thought his wig big enough already.

Other of his concerns also flourished during these years, for he was a founder member and Director of the Bank of England, and for three years a member of the Committee of the burgeoning East India Company. It can therefore be well appreciated that he was able to afford the purchase of a further 300 acres to add to his Tring deer park.

It is a pity that Sir William and his lady did not live long enough to enjoy their beautiful new surroundings, for Lady Gore, mother of eight surviving children, died in 1705 at the age of 52, and Sir William followed her less than three years later. His funeral cortège passed through the City of London, and he was buried in linen beside his wife.

Tring Park then passed to three Gore generations until 1786. Sir William's son (also William) should be remembered in the town as commissioning the Royal Gardener to re-model the grounds of Tring Park in a less rigid style. Thus evolved the naturalistic layout of the Park with which we are familiar today. More importantly to us, William changed the face of the town completely. Until 1711 the main road from London to Aylesbury passed on the south side of the Mansion. William objected to coaches rumbling past his dining-room windows, and petitioned that the road be re-directed. This request was granted, and the road now passes the Mansion on the north side, and at a level not visible to the house.

The new William 'beautified' the interior of the Parish Church, and Italian workmen painted the stone pillars in imitation of blue marble. Disliked by a later vicar, this was restored to the original, despite strident protests from parishioners who thought they might have to foot the bill. William also endowed £200 annually for a Charity School, and in 1718 initiated institutional Care for the Poor of Tring. Let us hope that the first Sir William would have been pleased with his son's efforts. Strangely, there is no monument in the church to William junior.

Sources

The Guildhall Library
'Nothing for Nothing for Nobody', Jack Parker 1986
Parish Magazines 1905 and 1906

Ruth Osborne achieved a dubious degree of fame only at the very end of her life when she was over seventy years of age. Such was the sensation caused that the villages around Tring all laid claim to her. Long Marston, Gubblecote, Puttenham, Wilstone, Marsworth, and Tring include her as part of their story. Little is known about her early life except that she was probably born in direst poverty in a cottage in the churchyard at Puttenham. Parish records show that her two children, William and Martha, were baptised at the church in the 1720s but by this time the Osbornes were living in the then 'Goblecourt'.

One day in 1745 Ruth called on a farmer named Butterfield who kept a dairy at Gubblecote, and begged for some buttermilk, but was roughly told he had not enough for his hogs. The nearly starving Ruth went away, calling back that The Pretender would have him - and his hogs too. (At that time the current 'bogeyman' was Bonnie Prince Charlie who was attempting to regain the throne for the Stuarts. He had recently led a serious rebellion and consequently was a figure of terror to the uneducated.) Shortly after this, several of Butterfield's calves died of distemper, rife at the time. This caused local ignorant folk to rumour that the animals had been bewitched by old mother Osborne. Fuel was added to the fire when Butterfield suffered a recurrence of the fits which troubled him at times. He became convinced that Ruth Osborne had put a curse on him, and surrounded his house with six men, armed with staves and pitchforks, and with charms around their necks to prevent further bewitching. These antics only drew more attention to the affair, and soon a group of mischief-makers put handbills round the district, announcing that Ruth and John Osborne were to be tried as witches at Long Marston on 22 April 1751. (Witchcraft had ceased to be a statutory offence by the passage of a Parliamentary Bill in 1736, but earlier efforts to discourage attacks upon poor women suspected of any mystic practice had failed. Mob violence of this sort still occurred spasmodically.)

With good reason the Parish Overseer, Matthew Burton, became seriously alarmed and had the Osbornes moved to Tring Workhouse for their own protection. Feelings still ran high, and the Master of this institution, Jonathan Tompkins, decided to move them to the even safer vestry of Tring Church. The next day a mob, said to number over 4,000, gathered outside the workhouse, frenziedly pulling down the pales, breaking the windows, and even ransacking the building. They seized Tompkins and threatened to drown him, and fire the town with the straw they had ready. The wretched man had no choice but to surrender the Osbornes to the mob. Ruth and John Osborne were then stripped naked, covered with a sheet with their thumbs and big toes tied together, and taken to Wilstone where for three-quarters of an hour they were held at *The Half Moon.* A muddy stream nearby was unblocked in readiness for their Ordeal by Ducking. Thomas Colley, a local chimney-sweep, considerably the worst for drink, then became ring-leader of the ghastly proceedings. Ruth and her husband were each dragged three times through the stream, and prodded and turned with a stick by Colley. Ruth, by then naked and choked with mud, expired on the bank within minutes but her husband, although severely bruised, still survived. Colley then

The Half Moon, Wilstone. c.1905

went round with his hat 'as a reward for the great pains he had taken in showing them sport'. The gang took Ruth and John and, unbeknown to the landlord, deposited them in his own bed in *The Half Moon*.

At Ruth's inquest a verdict of murder was returned against Thomas Colley, and he was committed for trial at the County Assizes at Hertford. The gruesome evidence of the many witnesses that were called was enough to prove his guilt, and he was formally condemned to execution, then hanged in chains at the spot where the crime was committed. In the custom of the day, on the gibbet he fully repented his sins declaring 'I do not believe there is such a thing in being as a witch'. He beseeched his audience to take heed of his words, but they remained unimpressed, and mutterings were heard to the effect that it was a hard case to hang a man for destroying a wicked old woman who had done so much mischief by her witchcraft. This thinking continued locally throughout the last years of John Osborne. Being some years younger than his wife, he was still able-bodied but found that no neighbouring farmer would employ him. They believed him still capable of wizardry, and John was compelled to become an inmate of Tring Workhouse for the remainder of his life.

Sources

    'The Gentleman's Magazine' Vol. XXI, 1751
    'Hertfordshire Countryside'

It is a pity that Karl Jordan was always viewed in Tring as very much a foreigner. He tried hard to assimilate, becoming naturalised in 1911, being always appreciative of the English way of life, and choosing to remain in Tring during his retirement. Maybe the reason why Karl was not fully accepted was that the jingoist years of the 1914 war, and his thick German accent, made local people uneasy. Neither did he achieve the full recognition in academic circles that his years of conscientious work at the Zoological Museum merited; this was acknowledged by many of his peers in the field of Entomology. If he had not chosen to spend his working life in Tring (then regarded as a back-water) this probably would not have occurred. Karl however did enjoy many advantages in life, including a happy marriage, superb mental and physical health, and a handsome appearance. Even that rather austere person, Lady Rothschild, commented that 'he was so extraordinarily good-looking'.

Karl Jordan was what would today be described as 'head-hunted' but in 1893 termed as 'invited' to join the staff of Tring Museum, by Walter Rothschild, then 24 years old. This proved an inspired choice, as no person more fitted for the task could be imagined. A frugal but happy childhood on a small farm just south of Hildesheim had formed a character of single-mindedness, and at an early age he displayed academic promise. Encouraged by an older brother, Karl soon started collecting and studying animals, plants, and especially, insects. This last became something of an obsession and decided his whole future. In 1886 he took his degree in Zoology and Botany. After marriage and five years teaching at a grammar school in Münden, came a post at the School of Agriculture in Hildesheim. Then the invitation to Tring followed.

At the Museum a strange state of affairs greeted Karl. 300,000 beetles which he had been engaged to classify and arrange were stored in fearful confusion in sheds and hired rooms scattered about Tring. Equally disconcerting was the lack of working space, and absence of a microscope. Amazingly, within a year this collection was in complete order. All this was achieved by Karl's enthusiasm, and the fact that he frequently worked 14 hours a day, returning to the Museum after dinner. There he was often joined by his wife, who helped with the labelling, possibly in the belief 'if you can't beat them, join them'.

Karl Jordan established a close rapport with Charles Rothschild, Walter's younger brother. This shy young man, who was also a gifted naturalist, responded to Karl's knowledgeable encouragement, both sharing characteristics of modesty, reserve and unselfishness.

Karl Jordan

When Charles became desperately ill in 1916 after an attack of influenza, Karl willingly left his family at Walter's request, and accompanied Charles to Switzerland in an attempt to assist his recovery. Sadly this was in vain, as Charles's illness eventually worsened and he died in 1923. When Karl returned home he met fresh trouble, finding his wife was suffering from renal disease, a condition from which she did not recover, dying in 1925. Understandably, he never adjusted fully to these tragedies, and he became withdrawn and threw himself even more strenuously into his work.

Much more could be written about Karl Jordan's career; for example he wrote over 460 papers, most of these publications concerning the systematics and distribution of beetles, butterflies, moths and fleas. He was made a Fellow of the Royal Society, and the Jordan Medal was founded in his memory in the United States.

Two reminders of Karl remain in Tring. One is the double-fronted white house in Park Road, still called *Jordans*, where he lived before moving to *Hildene* (now the site of St. Joseph's Retirement Home) in Aylesbury Road. The other is the Karl Jordan Room on the ground floor of the Walter Rothschild Museum in Akeman Street. This would have pleased Karl, as it was where he spent so many absorbing and happy hours during his lifetime.

Sources

    'Karl Jordan, A Biography', Royal Entomological Society 1955
    'Dear Lord Rothschild', Miriam Rothschild 1988

People in Tring are unlikely to know the name of Robert Hill, yet he certainly deserves to be remembered, for small country towns such as ours do not often produce such outstanding home-grown scholars, let alone one who was entirely self-taught.

Robert was born in 1699 at Miswell, which was then a hamlet of Tring. His parents were poor, and his father died soon after his birth. About five years later his mother married Thomas Robinson, a tailor in Buckingham. Robert was left at Miswell in the care of his grandmother, Mrs Clark. This lady must have had her grandson's best interests at heart for she taught him to read, and sent him to school for seven or eight weeks to learn the art of writing.

In 1710 Mrs Clark and Robert moved to Tring Grove where he became a farmer's boy. It very soon became apparent that his constitution was not sufficiently robust to follow the plough in the rough agricultural practices of the time. A new plan was devised whereby, in 1714, he joined his mother in Buckingham and became apprenticed to his step-father as a tailor. Here a chance gift changed Robert's life for ever. He was given two books - a Grammar and three-quarters of Littleton's Dictionary. These volumes fired his imagination and created an obsessive desire to read, and to learn. His first studies were in French and Latin, the latter for no other reason than to be able to read the epitaphs in the local church. As his master would not allow him free time from his work, he procured candles to enable him to read at night.

In 1717 Buckingham town was struck by an outbreak of smallpox, so Robert went back to Tring Grove to tend sheep on his uncle's farm. He is said to have lain all day under a hedge, reading through his library, which consisted of 'The Practice of Piety'. 'The Whole Duty of Man', and a French Grammar. When it was safe Robert returned to Buckingham, and with the help of the boys in the Free School, was able to continue his studies. In 1721 he married, but now aged 24 he found it hard to support a family by tailoring, so became a schoolmaster. His new profession proved something of a challenge. A pupil enrolled who had previously learnt about decimals, and because Robert's own experience of mathematics was small, in the short space of six weeks he made himself a master of proportional arithmetic. His reputation spread locally and his school soon numbered more than 50 scholars. This new-found career was not to last. First, Robert lost his wife, and then remarried in 1730. We are told this new wife was very 'unsatisfactory', but in what way is not explained.

Robert realised that he could not live with her, and he decided to leave home and travel the country. Having previously studied Greek, he next worked at Hebrew. This drove him to despair, as he considered that he was unable to master the proper phonetic pronunciation of the language, so he impetuously parted with his Hebrew books (an act which he was to regret later when he returned to study, and master, the subject).

The news of his second wife's death brought him back to Buckingham very swiftly, where he resumed his original profession of tailor and stay-maker. Undeterred by his previous matrimonial experiences, Robert wed for a third time in 1747. At about this time he came to the notice of a learned clergyman who was so impressed by him that he took Robert into his employment, and engaged him to write Observations on 'An Essay on the Spirit' by Bishop Berkley. This became the first of his works to be printed. A steady stream of erudite books and tracts followed, all of which are entirely unreadable today, but were greatly admired at the time. One title alone will suffice to explain this - 'Christianity the True Religion, an Essay in answer to the Blasphemy of the Deist'. During these productive literary years he was supported by a number of benevolent admirers, but by 1775 he was again in financial difficulties. In the quaint wording of the time 'learning and ingenuity have not been able to set him above the frowns of fortune'. These proved true words indeed, as Robert endured a long final illness before dying in Buckingham in 1777. Despite a life of poverty, struggle, and contrast, the fine mental ability of this Tring farmer's boy helped him to achieve general recognition.

Sources

Parish Magazine, October 1906
Dictionary of National Biography, Vol I

Several businesses have survived for about a century in Tring, and none more successfully than the operation started when in 1850 William Mead farmed some land, and developed a Milling business. William and his wife were born in Tring, and his decision to become a miller was well chosen, as was his use of an existing windmill at New Mill, and a wharf on a branch of the Grand Junction Canal at its highest point. This gave direct access to barges and provided easy loading and distribution of corn and flour. This fine planning ensured that the name MEAD soon became synonymous with flour-milling, and remained so.

Those barges which were loaded with hay and straw, bound for London, returned empty, so arrangements were made to bring back what was euphemistically called 'night soil' from the city, to be spread on the fields of local farmers.

There is some indication that by around 1861 the output of flour had become so high that a steam engine had to be installed to supplement the wind power. At that date the mill was run by William's younger son, Edward, who also rented the windmill at Wendover. He was a very busy man, with interests at Bury Mill, Watford; Piccotts End Mill; Hunton Bridge Mill; and at Chelsea

The Flour Mill at Gamnel, New Mill. c.1913

Flour Mill. His older brother, Thomas had also been hard at work expanding the business, and around 1868 he took control of the mill at Gamnel.

The business continued to grow through the years, and 1875 in particular was to prove a milestone in the story of Tring Flour Mill, when Thomas Mead decided on the erection of a 5-storey brick building alongside the existing windmill. A beam engine was installed in the new structure, and this was able to drive four pairs of millstones. Each success bred another. For 25 years a local family, the Bushells, had worked for the Meads, repairing and building the narrow boats used for transport of the corn and flour, but now they founded their own business alongside the Mead site. This logical development gave Bushell's the improved resources necessary to extend their activities into building all types of craft for canal and river use. This too was a story of success, and flourished until 1952.

Thomas Mead, meanwhile, constantly examined more ways to strengthen his milling operation, and in 1894 a new roller system was installed, to run simultaneously with the existing windmill. (The old beam engine continued in use until 1905, when a Woodhouse-Mitchell steam engine was installed. In its turn this ran efficiently for many years, but the mill was finally converted to electric power in 1946.)

Thomas had a fine family of ten children, including five sons, Thomas, Duncan, Frank, Percy, and William. Young Thomas died when a schoolboy, and Duncan was killed whilst serving in the Boer War. Frank carried on a branch of the Mead business at Clifford Mills at Northampton, and Percy farmed at Gubblecote and Wilstone. In due course the mill at Gamnel passed to William, and he managed the firm well. At various times he also worked Old Manor Farm at Wingrave; Hospital Farm at Marsworth; and Silk Mill Farm at Tring. Opposite the family home William built for his daughter an unusual dwelling which he called *Old Timbers Cottage*, as it was made from wood previously used for narrow boats. This was thatched with a semi-circular gable and worthy of its unique gate of wrought-iron, which was initiated by his father Thomas, built by Grace's of Tring, and known as The Implement Gate (since moved to Marsworth). This became a local landmark, and was often photographed and reproduced as a postcard.

The Implement Gate, New Mill,
with William Mead's little daughter

William Mead's public-spirited activity was greatly admired. One example was his purchase in 1921 of a large hut from a local military hospital, and his supervision of its erection and adaptation as New Mill's Church of St. George.

As he had no sons the Mead name disappeared from the Tring milling scene when the firm was acquired by Heygates of Northampton in 1944. The Meads would be glad to know that fine flour is still being produced at Gamnel, and is the last such operation in the Dacorum area. It would certainly surprise them that this now requires no miller, as the whole process is run by a bank of computers elsewhere.

Sources

    '*The Berkhamsted Gazette*', 1954
    '*Hertfordshire Windmills & Windmillers*', Cyril Moore 1999

In 1874 William Sexton, pastor for the General Baptists of Tring, died, and Charles Pearce was asked to occupy the pulpit for three months at a remuneration of seven shillings and sixpence a week. He wrote his own tribute to the lost reverend with these words: 'Our beloved Pastor was suddenly summoned by his maker ...Nature seemed to sympathise for it was a dark, gloomy, and wet day. The town mourned. Blinds were drawn close down and shutters up at every shop. Notwithstanding the incessant rain, an immense crowd collected round his grave.' A hard act for a temporary substitute to follow no doubt, but that is exactly what Charles Pearce did with outstanding success for the next 46 years.

Charles had been brought up in the Baptist tradition, his father, Alfred, being a stalwart member of the church in Thame, where Charles was born. Whilst he was still a young man, Charles moved to Tring and established a drapery business in the High Street. When only 24 years of age he is shown in the Census Return as living on the premises with his wife Jane, her young niece, and two employees, a shop assistant aged 18, and a general servant aged 16.

His period as stand-in for the ministry at Tring proved so effective that in 1876 he was called to the permanent pastorate - and at a time that was to see many changes in the life of the Church, and which was later to include a world war. Tring General Baptists were then still using their original small chapel in Frogmore Street. This was an unsatisfactory situation, described by Charles Pearce in a dismal Victorian manner as 'standing partly in the road, the least noise outside drowning the voice inside. The place is so hot, water runs down the walls, and many have to leave, fainting. The ceiling is low ... a brass viol and trombone are used to start the singing ... the baptistry is filled with buckets'. An even earlier account describes it as 'one of the queerest, stuffiest, ugliest chapels you can conceive of'. Clearly something had to be done, and early in his ministry Charles set about the task with his usual energy. In 1884 he launched his first campaign for a new building. Vigorous fund-raising over many years was carried out before the foundation stone of the Lecture Hall was laid in 1886, and the memorial stone in the walls of the present church followed in 1889. This fine building on the brow of the hill in Tring High Street was designed in the Gothic style by Tring architect, William Huckvale.

Membership of the church grew steadily during the next few years and matters progressed well. A setback occurred in 1903 when Charles had a bad accident, falling from his tricycle when riding to Thame to visit his elderly father. Two years later, trouble of a different sort arose for, in company with fellow Pastors from Akeman Street and New Mill, he protested against payment of the Education Rate - one of the disabilities still suffered by Nonconformists at that time. For this Charles was called before the magistrates.

On a lighter side, Charles Pearce was Pastor during the great Edwardian heyday of the Church Bazaar. In May 1902 a splendid event was organised in aid of the debt remaining on the new organ.

The new Church and Manse, High Street. c.1902

We are told that the entrance behind the chapel was resplendent with flags and bunting, and the recently-fitted hat pegs in the lobby were found to be a great convenience (provision of other 'conveniences' delicately is not mentioned). The hall itself was prettily decorated with national flags. Behind the platform were portraits of the King and Queen, tastefully draped with flags and art muslin in two harmonious shades. Lady Rothschild was to have opened the bazaar, but illness prevented this. Her Ladyship softened this blow by arranging instead a donation of the then large sum of £20 (which drew great applause from the assembled audience).

When this golden era ended, Charles faced what were some of the greatest challenges of his long career. Along with many others, the Great War moved him to despair, and for a man of his kindly heart the sufferings and deaths were hard to endure. In January 1915 he was nominated by the Army Board to serve as Chaplain for Tring, ministering to the soldiers billeted in the town; visiting the various military hospitals; and comforting those on leave, as well as grieving relatives mourning the loss of their menfolk. At onset of war Tring classrooms were requisitioned to hold billeted troops, and Charles Pearce was first in the town to offer the chapel's Lecture Hall as accommodation for the displaced children.

Charles was held in high affection by his congregation, and others in the town who came into contact with him. The last years of his ministry were not easy, for he endured a long period of failing eyesight. Care and thought were exercised towards him by his flock and they arranged that sloping aisles were constructed in the church to eliminate the steep steps. A member (James Clark) also regularly went with him into the pulpit to read the scripture. When Charles Pearce died in 1920 he was mourned deeply and sincerely, a tribute to the man who was engaged for three months, but stayed for 46 years.

Sources

> *'The Bucks Herald' archives*
> *'Short History of Tring United Free Church', Trevor Wright 1950*

On the front of the card designed for Dorian Williams' memorial service in Tring Church in 1985 his family selected a line from *II Corinthians, Ch IX* 'God Loveth a Cheerful giver': they thought this best summed up his character. All who knew him in Tring and elsewhere surely agreed. His 71 years of life were packed with non-stop activity and challenge, and in this he had a strong advantage, for he was able to bring to bear a natural and attractive quality - an enthusiasm for all that life had to offer.

Dorian's father was brought up at *Pendley Manor* (a property left to him later by his uncle Joseph Grout Williams), and his mother Violet was a daughter of Canon Wood, Rector of Aldbury. Dorian was born at Aldershot where his father, a cavalry officer, was stationed. Later the family moved to Greens Norton in Northants. Dorian and his brother and sister often spent happy school holidays with their grandparents at Aldbury, and these times bred in Dorian a love of the areas around Tring, which he retained for the rest of his life.

He admits that his visits to Pendley were far less enjoyable. The children were expected to meet the exacting standards demanded by their great-aunt Catherine, wife of their 'Uncle Joe'. (Joseph had acquired the Pendley estate in the 1870s, and built an impressive house in a vaguely 'Jacobethean' architectural style. In 1944 the property passed to Dorian). In one of his many books Dorian comments that he was grateful to have had the experience of a great estate in the days when such establishments were lavishly maintained. The tennis parties, family prayers, carriages, stables, and footmen, were all becoming part of a way of life that was rapidly passing away.

Dorian's education was basically upper-class until the time he left Harrow School. At that point he followed an unusual path, attending the Guildhall School of Music, but any ambitions this may have given him to sing or 'go on the stage' were cut short when he inherited a prep. school at Westgate-on-Sea. Despite his youth Dorian decided to become its headmaster and ran the school until the end of the war. (The acting and teaching talents he had learnt were soon to be brought to good use.) This period had been momentous for Dorian. In 1942 he contracted a serious illness from which he did not fully recover until 1944. His prolonged convalescence gave Dorian time to ponder how he would now develop Pendley, which had been run down during its wartime use by the Women's Land Army.

He decided to establish there a Centre for Adult Education. This concept was the first such in the country - and soon copied in other counties in Britain. Many difficulties needed to be overcome. It was essential to furnish and equip the house, ready to open as soon as the war finished. Most of Pendley's furniture had been sold to meet death duties, and new furniture was not easily obtainable. His 'action' character now came into full play: he formed a Board of Governors, which included the Bishop of St. Albans, the local M.P. Lady Davidson, and influential figures in the field of education. They were to raise the necessary finances, and they duly did; the syllabus was decided and the plan grew rapidly to fruition. The Centre was opened on a glorious autumn day in 1945. As well as recreational subjects, many students were sponsored by local authorities and industry. Very soon eighty different courses were offered for 3,000 regular students a year. This operation having been very successfully established, Dorian turned to something else which interested him, for in 1949 he finally exploited his love of theatre, by founding an immensely popular open-air Shakespeare Festival.

Responsible for over 50 productions of 26 different plays by the Bard, before an estimated audience of a quarter of a million people, Dorian made a cameo appearance in each play - often on horseback. The Festival became the highlight of the Pendley year, but was never allowed to override the main objective of the Centre, that of Adult Education - and the Shakespeare Festival continues successfully to this day.

He was devoted to horses and wrote about them as a journalist. He became Joint Master of the Grafton Hounds in 1951 and later took over as M.F.H. of the Whaddon Chase. But at times his great enthusiasm for fox-hunting exacted a price. His property was set on fire by groups of animal-rights protesters; he was often heckled and shouted down whilst giving talks on show-jumping; and at his memorial service at Tring Church some anti-hunt supporters gathered in a peaceful demonstration. At times Dorian admitted that the sport was controversial, but tried never to get involved in arguments on the subject.

He held office in many societies, including serving for 10 years as Chairman of the British Horse Society, and he was Master of the Worshipful Company of Farriers. He was awarded the O.B.E. in 1978 for his service to the world of the Horse.

The public best remembered 'Mr Horse' (as he became known) for his commentaries on television at 'The Horse of the Year Show'.

Dorian Williams talks with another Tring Personality,
show-jumper Pat Moss

His success in this topic was probably created by his uniquely frank, simple yet informative explanation of show-jumping, a subject which gave the opportunity for his mass audience to understand fully for the first time. This part of his career reached its apex with his popular commentaries on equestrian events in the various post-war Olympic Games.

Dorian always made time for local affairs, and his help was constantly sought, and given. His Directing skills were regularly requested for local entertainments. Long lists of such events could be detailed, of which the following are just two examples: In the 1950s he organised an annual Festival of Speech and Drama, at which local dramatic societies were invited to submit one-act plays of their choice. These were acted out and adjudicated upon in the drawing room at Pendley. In 1966, by request, he staged and directed a Pageant in the Berkhamsted Castle grounds, which celebrated the 900th anniversary of the offer of the Crown of England to William the Conqueror. This too was a spectacular success.

He always reacted sympathetically to local problems. When the Tring Town Football Club lost its pitch he provided a field on his estate which adjoined Cow Lane. He was invited to, and became, the Club's President. He took an active interest in its fortunes, and then made over, at a peppercorn rent of £1 a year, 28 acres adjacent to this pitch to be used for other ball sports. This is now the Pendley Sports Centre Ltd. and includes the Rugby, Squash, and Bowls clubs.

Like everyone, Dorian had his share of setbacks and grief. He had an early marriage that failed; the death of his brother in World War II (accidentally shot by bullets from one of the tanks he commanded) caused Dorian to comment 'I have known no sadness to compare with that I experienced when Maurice died.' Also the comparatively early death of his mother may have helped him to prepare for his own ordeal ahead, for in 1972 Dorian faced cancer cheerfully, and with candour. Despite three operations and painful treatment he continued normal life, by adding a full-time Pendley manager, but this proved to be unsatisfactory, for by 1981

Dorian Williams performs the opening ceremony of the new
premises at Tring Town F.C. in August 1975

a financial crisis was looming. After much heart-searching and
discussion Dorian made the decision to dispose of Pendley.

The Adult Education Centre carried on for a time, but later this
became an hotel. In July 1985 Dorian died at his home, *Foscote
Manor* in Buckinghamshire, leaving second wife Jennifer and two
children, Piers and Carola. At his own request, his ashes were
scattered over the grassy area of the Shakespeare Festival open-air
stage at Pendley.

Sources

    'Pendley and a Pack of Hounds', *Dorian Williams 1959*
    'Master of One', *Dorian Williams 1978*
    'Between the Lines', *Dorian Williams 1984*
    'The Times', *July 1985*